CW00350684

CANCER

THE ASTROSEX SERIES

CANCER

*How to have the best sex
according to your star sign*

ERIKA W. SMITH

First published in Great Britain in 2021 by Orion Spring
an imprint of The Orion Publishing Group Ltd
Carmelite House, 50 Victoria Embankment
London EC4Y 0DZ

An Hachette UK Company

1 3 5 7 9 10 8 6 4 2

Text by Erika W. Smith
Illustrations by Laura Brett
Copyright © The Orion Publishing Group 2021

A CIP catalogue record for this book is available from the British Library.

ISBN (Hardback) 9781398702004
ISBN (eBook) 9781398702011

Printed and bound in Great Britain by Clays Ltd, Elcograf, S.p.A

www.orionbooks.co.uk

ORION
SPRING

CONTENTS

1

ASTROLOGY:
AN INTRODUCTION

Sometime in the past fifty years, astrology-related flirtation went from 'Hey, baby, what's your sign?' to 'So, what time *exactly* were you born?' Thanks to the Internet, it's easier than it's ever been to pull up your crush's entire birth chart online and see how it compares to your own. I'll let you decide if this is a good thing or a bad thing.

But our fascination with astrology is nothing new. Humans have charted the movements of the Sun and Moon as far back as the Stone Age. Experts disagree on when precisely 'Ooh, look at the Moon!' turned into using the planets to predict the future, but it's clear that the practice has been around for thousands of years. Modern astrology dates back to ancient Babylonian times, with the first references to it arising somewhere in the second or third millennium BCE and the first recorded birth chart appearing around 410 BCE; Chinese astrology dates back even earlier.

In fact, astrology is so old that when it began astrologers believed the Earth was flat. And although we've long since learned better, astrology still charts the movement of the planets as they appear from *our* perspective on solid ground. When we talk about 'Mercury retrograde' – the much-hyped period of time when Mercury wreaks havoc on our lives by messing up our technology, causing us to miscommunicate and prompting our exes to send us a 2 a.m. 'sup?' text – we're referring to when Mercury is moving backwards in its orbit *from our point of view on Earth*. Mercury isn't suddenly defying the laws of gravity and reversing its course around the Sun; its apparent backwards motion is a trick of perspective caused by the different speeds of Mercury's and Earth's orbits. Have you ever looked out of the window in a fast-moving car and seen a slower-moving car appear to move backwards? Yeah, it's like that. (If you try this at home, have someone else drive – and watch the speed limit!)

So, does this mean that astrology is fake? I've broken my phone or missed my train during Mercury retrograde too many times to say yes. But, in my opinion, 'Is astrology real?' isn't the point – the planets don't care what you think about them. You don't have to believe that your day-to-day life mirrors the movements of the Universe to find astrology a useful tool in your life, or even just an interesting subject. Astrology has been around literally for millennia, through countless ebbs and flows in perceived legitimacy and popularity in different cultures and different interpretations. So, if you ask your next Tinder match what their sign is and they're all, 'Why do people believe in that junk?' – well, astrology will survive long after you've forgotten they existed. (Also, don't bother arguing; just unmatch them. Or, if you want to have fun, just say, 'Oh, you must be a Capricorn'.)

You probably first became familiar with astrology through horoscopes – looking up your sign in a newspaper or magazine to see what might happen that day/week/month. But your sign is just one part of your birth chart. Although it's often called your 'star sign', the proper astrological term is your **Sun sign**. It's determined by the placement of the Sun when you were born. But you also have a sign describing where the Moon was when you were born, and Mars, and Venus, and Jupiter, and every other planet in the sky – not to mention asteroids like Chiron and mathematical points like the Nodes of Destiny (see page 63 if you can't wait to find out what these are). Yeah, it's complicated!

The more you learn about astrology, the more there is to find out – if there's a point where you know it all, I'm certainly nowhere near finding it.

Astrology can be used to predict your future, yes, but it can also be used to help you understand yourself. I'm a Scorpio, an intense sign that represents sex, death, transformation and the occult. But as a shy, awkward pre-teen first learning about astrology, I thought that didn't sound much like me at all. I felt more like a philosophical, travel-loving Sagittarius, the sign after Scorpio – and when I got older and learned more about astrology, I found out that my Moon, Mercury and Venus are all in Sagittarius, so my connection with that sign makes total sense (though these days I completely embrace my Scorpio traits).

In this book, you'll learn the basics of reading your birth chart, and then go deep into the fun part: what astrology tells you about sex and compatibility. If you're already an astrology know-it-all, feel free to skip ahead to Part III (to page 67, to be exact), but if you're a newbie to the stars or just want a refresher, then this first section is for you. On the other hand, if you can't wait to get to the sexy stuff, go for it and then come back to this part later to learn more about the nitty-gritty details.

Astrology contains a lot of its own language – words like 'trine', 'mutable' and 'modality'. But while these words can be confusing at first, they're usually used to describe fairly easy-to-understand concepts – and as you read more about astrology, you'll probably find yourself using the lingo, too. If you get confused, though, take a look at the Glossary on page 125 – we've marked terms listed there in bold on their first use.

2

HOW TO READ
YOUR BIRTH CHART

Think of your birth chart (sometimes called your 'natal chart') as a snapshot of what the sky looked like at the moment you were born. Each planet, asteroid and mathematical point aligns with a certain zodiac sign – and each placement plays a role in describing your personality and your future. In fact, some astrologers say that you shouldn't share your birth chart, because it reveals so much about you! (So think twice before posting a screenshot on Instagram.)

Although the Sun stays in one sign for a full month, the Moon changes signs approximately every two and a half days, and your Rising sign (also called Ascendant) – which describes which sign was on the eastern horizon when you arrived on Earth – changes about every two *hours*. This is why there are so many jokes about texting your mum

11

to find out your birth time – whether you were born at 6 a.m. or 6 p.m. can make a big difference in your chart. Knowing the location of your birth is similarly important. The sky at 6 a.m. in London looks very different from the sky at 6 a.m. in Tokyo on the same day.

Once you know your birth time and location, it's a simple step to calculate your birth chart. Pre-internet, you'd have had to go to a professional astrologer to have them draw one up for you – but these days, you can get it calculated in just a few seconds on many free websites and apps. I like the app TimePassages and the website Cafe Astrology, but there are plenty of options out there.

What if I don't know my birth time?

There are many reasons why you might not know your exact birth time – for example, you may be adopted and not have a record of your exact time of birth; you may be estranged from your birth family; or you may have been born in a country that doesn't record birth times on your birth certificate. If you don't know your birth time, there are a few options when calculating your birth chart:

- Put your birth time as 12 p.m. Noon is halfway through the day, so this gives you an 'average' of where the planets and zodiac signs may have been. This is called a 'noon chart'.

- Visit an astrologer for something called a 'natal chart rectification'. The astrologer will ask you questions about your personality and significant events in your life. This helps them essentially work backwards to figure out the uncertain parts of your birth chart.

- Focus on what you do know. Although you need your birth time to find out your Rising sign, houses and sometimes your Moon sign, you can find out many other placements with just a birth date.

Your birth chart can look confusing at first glance, but once you break it down into smaller pieces, it's easier to read. Think of the circle as describing a bird's-eye view of the cosmos at the moment you were born. The outer circle shows the symbols of the twelve zodiac signs, the middle circle is divided into 360 degrees and shows the placement of each planet within a zodiac sign (something we won't get into here), the inner circle shows the twelve houses and the lines in the middle point out the **aspects** – or angles, which indicate a certain kind of energy – between the planets. The symbols scattered in the middle represent the different planets in your birth chart. So if you're looking for your Moon sign, for example, you'd look for the Moon symbol (which looks, helpfully, like a little crescent moon). Once you've found it, see which sign and house it falls in. If you want to go even deeper, follow the lines to see what kind of relationship each planet has with other parts of your birth chart.

Still sounds complicated? Most birth-chart calculators will simply list your placements (and sometimes aspects) as well as showing you the chart, so you can just read them (and print them out or save them to your phone, because you'll likely want to come back to check them!). Here's an example chart for someone born in London, on 7 April 1992, at 6:05 a.m.

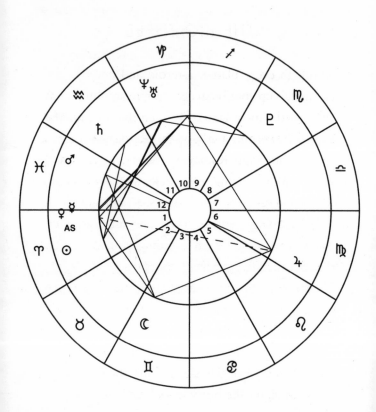

THE BIG THREE

Although every planet, asteroid and point in the sky makes up your birth chart, there are three signs that get the most focus. I've seen them compared to the Powerpuff Girls or the Kardashian sisters (Kim, Khloé and Kourtney – sorry, Kendall and Kylie). We're talking, of course, about your Sun, Moon and Rising signs. If you see a Tinder bio with three astrology emojis listed one after another, that's what your match is telling you. Each sign describes a different part of your personality. When I was first getting into astrology, a friend helpfully explained them to me as 'your self, your drunk self and the self people think you are'.

Your Sun sign: **Your Sun sign is your 'star sign' or 'main' sign – the one you look up when you read your horoscope or when you picked up this book. It's determined by the placement** of the Sun when you were born, AKA your birthday. It describes your basic identity and your life purpose – yeah, NBD!

Your Moon sign: **Your Moon sign** describes where the Moon was when you were born. The Moon changes signs more frequently than the Sun – every two or three days compared to roughly once a month. Your Moon sign represents your needs and desires and how you experience emotions. As my friend joked, it's the side of you that might come out when you're drunk, or simply tired or stressed.

Your Rising sign: **Your Rising sign**, also called your **Ascendant**, is determined by the sign that was rising on the eastern horizon when you were born. It changes every few hours. It describes the 'mask' you show the world – the way you present yourself to others, particularly people you don't know well, and the first impressions

18

you make. I have a close friend whose Sun sign is Capricorn – meaning she's ambitious, driven and a hard worker. And that checks out, but she's also super extroverted and hilarious – which makes sense, as her Rising sign is in exuberant Leo.

THE OTHER PLANETS

Every part of your birth chart is important, but some planets play a bigger role in your day-to-day life than others. The inner planets – the Sun, Moon, Mercury, Venus and Mars – are sometimes called the 'personal planets' because they describe different aspects of your personality. They change signs often, spending anywhere from two weeks (Mercury) to two months (Mars) in one sign. Think of it this way: the people in your class at school had a wide range of different Sun, Moon, Mercury, Venus and Mars signs.

The middle planets – Jupiter and Saturn – are sometimes called 'social planets'. They 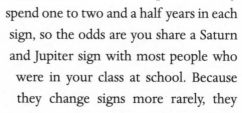 spend one to two and a half years in each sign, so the odds are you share a Saturn and Jupiter sign with most people who were in your class at school. Because they change signs more rarely, they describe bigger themes of your life, rather than your day-to-day feelings and instincts.

Finally, the outer planets – Uranus, Neptune and Pluto – stay in one sign anywhere from seven to thirty *years*. They're sometimes called 'generational planets' because they describe themes that affect entire generations. Most people in your entire university likely had the same Uranus, Neptune and Pluto signs.

When it comes to your sex life, the Sun, Moon, Venus and Mars play the biggest roles – and Mercury is also important, because Mercury represents communication and you need to communicate to have sex! So, pay special attention to the inner planets in your birth chart, although we can look to the outer planets to explain changing norms around sex and dating from generation to generation.

Here's what each planet represents in your birth chart:

Sun: **The Sun represents your identity and your life's purpose.**

Moon: **The Moon represents your emotions, your needs and your subconscious thoughts and desires.**

Mercury: **Often called the 'messenger planet', Mercury represents how you communicate and express yourself.**

Venus: Sometimes called 'the planet of love',
Venus represents how you experience romance,
money, beauty and pleasure.

Mars: Named for the god of war, Mars represents
your energy, how you take action, how you
fight and how you experience desire – including
your sex drive.

Jupiter: Jupiter represents how you experience
good luck, personal growth and big ideas like
philosophy and religion.

Saturn: Often described as a taskmaster, Saturn represents your sense of responsibility and ambition.

Uranus: The planet of disruption and revolution, Uranus represents how you rebel and create change in your life.

Neptune: Sometimes called 'the planet of dreams and illusions', Neptune represents your fantasies, dreams and intuition.

Pluto: Named for the god of the underworld, Pluto represents rebirth and transformation.

Do you have a stellium? If you have three or more planets in the same sign, you have a stellium. Even if your Sun is in a different sign, the sign in which you have the majority of your placements will play a big role in your personality – especially if it's mostly the inner planets. For example, maybe your Sun is in Libra, but your Mercury, Venus and Mars are all in Scorpio. If you have a stellium, you might want to give it a glance when you read your horoscope, too.

EACH SIGN'S
PERSONALITY TRAITS

Each sign has unique personality traits that are associated with it and they don't only show up in your Sun sign. If your Sun is in Sagittarius and your Mars is in Capricorn, you're very adventurous and philosophical – but when it comes to taking action, fighting or pursuing what you want, you've got a very methodical approach.

Here are some of each sign's most well-known traits, as well as the animal or object that represents it. For fun, we've also added some celebs who share your sign – but don't write in to complain if you're not happy with the comparison!

Aries: The Ram
21 March–19 April

As the first sign of the zodiac, Aries is both the leader and the baby. They're known for being passionate, impulsive, courageous and blunt. They have a playful nature and although they have hot tempers, they don't hold grudges.

Celebrity Aries: Lady Gaga, Reese Witherspoon, Mariah Carey, Diana Ross, Chaka Khan

Taurus: The Bull
20 April–20 May

Taurus is slow and steady compared to hotheaded Aries. These bulls work hard to get what they want, but they also value their downtime and have an appreciation for the finer things in life. They're also incredibly stubborn

– don't try to argue with one, because you won't win.

Celebrity Taureans: George Clooney, Gigi Hadid, Channing Tatum, David Beckham, Dev Patel

Gemini: The Twins
21 May–20 June

Geminis are often described as being two personalities in one person. They're super smart, talkative and creative – they tend to be social butterflies. They also tend to be moody, so don't be surprised if your Gemini friend acts as sweet as sugar one day and is withdrawn the next.

Celebrity Geminis: Kanye West, Naomi Campbell, Angelina Jolie, Mary-Kate and Ashley Olsen

Cancer: The Crab
21 June–22 July

Crabs carry their houses on their backs with them, so naturally Cancers are all about the idea of home. They tend to be very particular about how they decorate their places, and they want to take care of their loved ones. However, they'll strike out with their claws if provoked.

Celebrity Cancerians: Ariana Grande, Lana Del Rey, Selena Gomez, Jaden Smith, Meryl Streep

Leo: The Lion
23 July–22 August

Like the king of the jungle, Leos are natural leaders – and show-offs. They tend to be the life of the party, and they often have just a little bit of an ego.

But they're also incredibly loyal and generous. Leos are always there for their fans – er, friends.

Celebrity Leos: Madonna, Jennifer Lopez, Kylie Jenner, Meghan Markle, Mick Jagger

 Virgo: The Maiden
23 August–22 September

Virgo is represented by the virgin or the maiden, but that doesn't necessarily describe their sex life. (In fact, many Virgos present as innocent but have a not-so-secret dirty side.) Virgos are analytical, precise and logical – the ones who made sure that every group project got an A. They're very health-conscious (and can even be hypochondriacs) and like things to be neat.

Celebrity Virgos: Beyoncé, Keanu Reeves, Zendaya, Idris Elba, Colin Firth

Libra: The Scales
23 September–22 October

Represented by the scales, Libras are focused on justice ... but they also take forever to make a decision. They tend to be diplomatic and social. They're also aesthetically minded and tend to be fashionable and creative – not to mention flirtatious and charming.

Celebrity Librans: Kim Kardashian, Will Smith, Serena Williams, Gwyneth Paltrow

Scorpio: The Scorpion
23 October–21 November

Scorpios are known to be intense – their sign rules sex, death and the occult, after all. This witchy sign tends to be secretive; they come off as guarded until you know them well. They love learning others' secrets but are reluctant to share when it comes to their own, and they can be a little obsessive about the topics and people who interest them.

Celebrity Scorpios: Winona Ryder, Drake, Leonardo DiCaprio, Gabrielle Union

 Sagittarius: The Archer
22 November–21 December

Represented by an archer centaur, Sagittarians are adventurous and passionate. They love travelling and learning and tend to have a philosophical side to them. Haters say they're flaky, flighty and non-committal, but Sagittarians prefer independent, thank you very much.

Celebrity Sagittarians: Taylor Swift, Britney Spears, Jay-Z, Chrissy Teigen

Capricorn: The Sea-goat
22 December–19 January

Capricorns have big CEO energy. They're super logical, super ambitious and focused on the tangible things, like their bank balance and their job titles. They work hard and care deeply about security – both financial and emotional. They tend to have a dark, dry sense of humour, and they're very loyal to their loved ones.

Celebrity Capricorns: Michelle Obama, Denzel Washington, Kate Middleton, John Legend

Aquarius: The Water-bearer
20 January–18 February

Sometimes called 'the weirdos of the zodiac' or 'the robots of the zodiac', Aquarians tend to be a little quirky. They're likely to have offbeat interests and unusual hobbies – but they're also humanitarians, so as weird as they seem, all their work is a force for good. Aquarians are often described as loners – they're so focused on inventing their latest creation or plotting their new sci-fi novel that they tend to go off into their own worlds.

Celebrity Aquarians: Oprah Winfrey, Harry Styles, Justin Timberlake, Jennifer Aniston

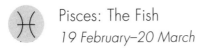

Pisces: The Fish
19 February–20 March

The last sign of the zodiac, Pisceans are wise and intuitive – in fact, some even say they're psychic. They are also emotional and romantic; they tend to get caught up in a fantasy, and their feelings get hurt easily. They're also artistic and creative, and empathetic towards others.

Celebrity Pisceans: Rihanna, Lupita Nyong'o, Drew Barrymore, Erykah Badu

What about Ophiuchus? Once a year or so, a story goes around saying that scientists have 'discovered' a new zodiac sign, Ophiuchus. Not so fast! Ophiuchus is a constellation in the sky, but it's not a new one – it was first identified in the second century. Astrologers have always known about it, but there are so many constellations in the sky that they decided to limit the zodiac to only twelve signs. Ophiuchus simply didn't make the cut – and neither did dozens of other constellations. As for the scientists? They practise astronomy, not astrology, which is a totally separate field. (As I unfortunately learned when I took an astronomy class at university ... spoiler alert, it was mostly physics and not astrology at all.)

PLANETARY RULERS

Each planet '**rules**' a sign – meaning that they share a similar energy and the planet feels most 'at home' in that sign (or, in astro-speak, '**in its domicile**'). Once you know your Sun sign's ruling planet, you'll want to pay close attention to what that planet's up to in the sky, because it will have an even stronger influence on you than on the rest of us.

If a planet is in the sign it rules – either in day-to-day life or in your birth chart – its energy is even more powerful. Some signs have more than one ruler; this is because when astrology first began, we didn't yet know that all of the outer planets existed!

Aries: Mars

Aries is ruled by Mars, which is all about action, passion and drive – which is a natural fit for this hotheaded fire sign.

Taurus: Venus

Taurus is ruled by Venus, the planet of love, pleasure and money – bulls can thank Venus for their love of luxury and their romantic streak.

Gemini: Mercury

It makes perfect sense that talkative Gemini is ruled by Mercury, the planet of communication. Mercury influences the Twins' way with words – not to mention their love of gossip.

Cancer: The Moon

The moodiest planet and the moodiest sign are, of course, a natural pair. The Moon and Cancer share an emotionality, a passion for nurturing others and a strong intuition.

Leo: The Sun

Like the Sun, Leo shines. They were born for the spotlight! They're also warm, nurturing, and might think the world revolves around them.

Virgo: Mercury

While Virgo isn't as social as Gemini, their ruling planet Mercury points to Virgo's precise, analytical mind – as well as their nervous energy.

Libra: Venus

Like Taurus, Libra is ruled by Venus. The planet of love is also the planet of beauty, and both make sense for typical Librans, who are as stylish as they are romantic.

Scorpio: Mars and Pluto

Lucky Scorpio has two ruling planets – Mars, which gives the scorpion a passion that can border on obsession, and Pluto, which influences their interest in all things dark and mysterious.

Sagittarius: Jupiter

Jupiter is sometimes called the planet of expansion, so of course it rules adventurous Sagittarius, who would visit a new country every week if they could. Jupiter is also to thank for the archer's boundless optimism and innate good luck.

Capricorn: Saturn

Saturn is the planet of structure, and Capricorn *loves* structure – not to mention discipline, hard work and responsibility, all of which Saturn governs.

Aquarius: Saturn and Uranus

Uranus is the planet of revolution, while Saturn is the planet of structure – and Aquarius is all about shaking up the status quo.

Pisces: Jupiter and Neptune

Pisceans have two ruling planets: Jupiter, which gives them optimism and luck, and Neptune, which explains their dreamy, head-in-the-clouds nature.

THE POLARITIES

Once you know all your different signs – your Sun sign, Moon sign, Mercury sign, etc. – it's time to get to know more about them. There are several ways that astrologers group the signs. One way is by polarity – active or receptive. The polarities used to be called 'masculine' and 'feminine', but I believe these divisions are on their way out as we've moved on from old-fashioned sexist ideas about gender. Some astrologers now refer to them as active and passive, inward-looking and outward-looking or positive and negative (like a magnet).

Active (Aries, Gemini, Leo, Libra, Sagittarius, Aquarius)

Active signs tend to be more outgoing and extroverted – they thrive when they're able to bounce ideas off other people. They tend to be optimistic, impulsive and assertive.

Receptive (Taurus, Cancer, Virgo, Scorpio, Capricorn, Pisces)

Receptive signs are usually more reserved and introverted – they value their alone time and they need to trust someone before they open up. They tend to be more pessimistic (or, as they might say, realistic), thoughtful and emotional.

THE ELEMENTS

Another way astrologers group signs is by **element**: fire, earth, air and water. The signs within these groups share common traits and tend to get along well, whether as friends, lovers or romantic partners. They also get along well with a certain other element – fire and air, earth and water (which makes sense … think of a bonfire and a garden). To learn more about yourself, look at your chart to see if you have a lot of planets in a certain element. Even if you're a fiery Leo Sun, if you have a lot of planets in water signs, you've probably got an emotional side lurking close to the surface.

 Fire (Aries, Leo, Sagittarius)

As you might expect by the name, fire signs are passionate and hotheaded. They tend to have tempers, and they tend to be impulsive. Their fiery personalities make them well suited to being leaders (or at least the life of the party).

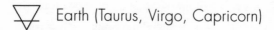 Earth (Taurus, Virgo, Capricorn)

Earth signs are grounded – they live in the here and now. They're practical, they plan ahead and you always want one on your team. They're all about the physical world, so they're very sensual – whether it's a good meal, a luxurious robe or amazing sex, they like things they can touch, feel and taste.

Air (Gemini, Libra, Aquarius)

Air signs tend to live in their heads – they're intellectuals or 'ideas people', and they often have a way with words, too. They're playful and quick-moving, and you always want one at your party. They also think a lot about aesthetics and how they appear to others, whether they're trying to become the centre of a social circle or proudly and happily standing alone.

 ## Water (Cancer, Scorpio, Pisces)

The stereotype about water signs is that they cry a lot, and as one, I have to say it's true! Water signs are emotional, and their feelings often get the better of them. They're also intuitive and introspective, not to mention nostalgic.

THE MODALITIES

You can also understand your planetary placements by looking at their **modality**. Astrologers group signs into three modalities: cardinal, fixed or mutable. These modalities describe where in the season each sign falls, which of course corresponds to certain personality traits. Similar to the elements, look at your whole birth chart to get an idea of your vibe. You might be a stubborn Taurus, but if you have a lot of planets in mutable signs, you're probably more willing to work towards a compromise than some of your fellow bulls.

Cardinal (Aries, Cancer, Libra, Capricorn)

Cardinal signs fall at the beginning of a season and they tend to be leaders, thinkers and trendsetters.

Fixed (Taurus, Leo, Scorpio, Aquarius)

Fixed signs fall in the middle of the season. They tend to be stabilisers, planners and 'doers'. Also, they're stubborn AF.

Mutable (Gemini, Virgo, Sagittarius, Pisces)

Mutable signs fall at the end of a season, and they've brought the wisdom of their season with them. They're also adaptable and flexible.

YOUR RISING SIGN
AND THE HOUSES

Your Rising sign not only represents the face you show the world, it also determines where the **houses** in your birth chart fall. Each birth chart is divided up into twelve sections, called 'houses', and each house determines a certain broad area of your life – such as 'family' or 'career'. Your Rising sign always falls on the cusp of your first house.

There are several different house systems in astrology, but for simplicity's sake, we'll stick with the system called 'whole sign houses' here, in which each house perfectly aligns with one sign. Your Rising sign always aligns with your first house. Then, the sign after your Rising sign aligns with your second house, and so on. For example, if your Rising sign is Cancer, your first house would be in Cancer, your second house would be in Leo, your third house would be in Virgo, and so on and so on. On paper, it looks like the face of a clock, starting at 9 p.m. and moving around the clock counterclockwise.

Everyone's birth chart includes all twelve houses and all twelve signs. However, different people will have houses fall in different signs, and different planets fall in different signs and houses, too. For example, someone with a Cancer Rising might have her third house in Virgo, but her partner's third house might be in Scorpio, and her BFF's third house might be in Capricorn.

Like the planets, each house represents a different area of your life. In your birth chart, the sign your house aligns with describes the vibe that area of your life will have. For example, if your eighth house, which rules romance, is in Sagittarius, you likely have an adventurous sex life and prefer to date casually until you're 100 per cent certain you want to commit to someone.

Just like each sign has a ruling planet, each house has a ruling sign. This doesn't necessarily mean that this house will align with its ruling sign in your birth chart – but when it does, that area of your chart is supercharged.

Here's what area of your life each house rules:

First house: **First impressions, self-image, identity and appearance. Ruled by Aries.**

Second house: **Values, resources, possessions and money. Ruled by Taurus.**

Third house: **Communication, gossip, siblings, learning and short-distance travel. Ruled by Gemini.**

Fourth house: **Home, foundation, security, tradition and family. Ruled by Cancer.**

Fifth house: **Inspiration, romance, creativity and children. Ruled by Leo.**

Sixth house: Work, responsibilities, health, daily routine and pets. Ruled by Virgo.

Seventh house: Partnerships, marriage, contracts and open enemies. Ruled by Libra.

Eighth house: Sex, death, transformation and the occult. Ruled by Scorpio.

Ninth house: Education, philosophy, religion and long-distance travel. Ruled by Sagittarius.

Tenth house: Career, reputation, ambition and social standing. Ruled by Capricorn.

Eleventh house: Community, friendships and good fortune. Ruled by Aquarius.

Twelfth house: Secrets, loss, sorrow, spirituality and hidden enemies. Ruled by Pisces.

So, how does that relate to sex? Some of the houses – like the fifth and eighth houses – more clearly relate to sex and relationships than others. But that doesn't mean that the others play no role in your sex life. If you meet your SO at work, your sixth house might have had an influence; if you meet your boo on vacation, check out what's going on in your ninth house. You get the idea.

Empty and Full Houses

Every planet in your birth chart will be in both a sign and a house, but you'll have some signs and houses that don't have any planets in them – these are called 'empty houses'. There are only ten planets in your birth chart, after all (for astrology's sake, the Sun and Moon count as planets), so most people have at least two empty houses – and usually more.

If you have empty houses, the themes of those houses simply won't play a major role in the story of your life. For example, if your second house is empty, you might not be too concerned about finances because you've never had to worry about how you're going to pay rent.

If you do want to get some guidance on your empty house, look to the ruling planet for that house's sign. Sounds complicated? Let's say your sixth house of work is empty. It's ruled by Virgo, and Virgo is ruled by Mercury. Then look to the location of Mercury in your birth chart. If it's in, say, the fourth house, those areas of your life may be combined. The sixth house rules work, responsibility and daily routine, while the fourth house rules home, foundation and family – so you might work for a family business, or you might decide not to take a traditional nine-to-five in order to be a stay-at-home parent or caretaker for an older or ill relative, or you might work to pay the bills while your true passion in life is your family.

On the other hand, houses where you have many planets – 'full houses' – will appear in your life in a big way. If you have many planets in the third house of communication, writing or speaking will play a major role in your life – you may be a journalist or politician, you may teach sign language or be multilingual.

Putting It All Together

Now's the time to combine all this information. When you look at your birth chart, each planet is in both a sign and a house. Taken all together, these placements describe your personality and the course of your life. For example, my Scorpio (sign of sex, death and the occult) Sun (determining my personality and life's purpose) is in my third house of communication, so it's no surprise that I'm writing this book on sex and astrology.

WANT EVEN MORE?

Although this might seem like a lot of information, there's even more to your birth chart than what we just went over! While this is by no means exhaustive, here are a few other topics you might want to explore.

Aspects

Aspects are, to put it simply, the angles the planets in your chart make with each other. Certain angles have certain energies, so the planets may work together or against each other – thus revealing which areas of your life come naturally and which are a challenge. Here are some of the most important aspects, though there are other measurements, too (including one of my favourite astro-words, 'quincux' – meaning two planets that are 150 degrees apart).

Conjunction: Two (or more) planets are in the same sign; their energy is blended and they work together.

Sextile: Planets are 60 degrees apart, or two signs away from each other; this is a harmonious aspect, in which the two planets encourage each other.

Trine: Planets are 120 degrees apart, or four signs away from each other (and in the same element – for example, Pluto in Scorpio and Mercury in Pisces). This aspect is also harmonious and acts similarly to a sextile.

Square: Planets are 90 degrees apart, or three signs away from each other. This is a challenging aspect, in which there will be tension between the planets.

Opposition: Planets are 180 degrees apart, or six signs apart – they're opposite each other on the zodiac wheel. In an opposition, the two planets work against each other, as if they're playing tug-of-war.

Essential Dignity

Remember how each sign has a ruling planet? Each planet has a different level of comfort in each sign – something called 'essential dignity'. If it's in its ruling sign, we say it's in its domicile, when it's at its most powerful. But it can also be in its detriment, in which it has to work harder to have an impact. And, of course, there are several levels in between domicile and detriment!

Domicile: The sign in which a planet is most at home and has the most power.

Exaltation: The sign in which a planet feels particularly comfortable.

Fall: The sign in which a planet feels particularly uncomfortable.

Detriment: The sign in which a planet's influence is least powerful.

POINTS IN YOUR CHART

We've covered the planets and your Rising sign, but there are other parts of the Universe that appear in your birth chart – both physical objects, such as asteroids, and mathematical points, such as the Nodes of Destiny. Here are a few you may come across, and what they represent:

Asteroids

Eros: **What you're passionate about – including your turn-ons.**

Psyche: **Your relationship needs.**

Sappho: **Yearning for love.**

Ceres: **What you need to be healthy, and how you help others.**

Pallas: How you create change.

Juno: How you seek to right
    inequalities.

Vesta: Your higher purpose.

Chiron: Where you face emotional wounds.

Lilith: Areas of life you struggle with, and how you
    overcome them.

Points

Descendant (DSC): Remember how your Rising
    sign is sometimes called an Ascendant? You also
    have a Descendant, directly across from your
    Ascendant. Think of it as your 'shadow self'.

Midheaven (MC): Found on the cusp of your tenth
    house, your Midheaven describes your career
    and public self.

Imum Coeli (IC): **Found on the cusp of your fourth house and opposite your Midheaven, your *Imum Coeli* describes your roots and foundations.**

The Nodes of Destiny: **The Nodes of Destiny are two mathematical points determined by the angles between the Sun, Moon and Earth when you were born. The North Node represents what we need to work on for spiritual growth, and the South Node represents the areas of life that come to us easily. They're always 180 degrees from each other, or zodiacal opposites.**

OKAY, SO WHAT DOES ALL THIS HAVE TO DO WITH SEX?

Now that you've learned a little bit about your birth chart, we're going to dive deeper into sex and your Sun sign. But now you know that astrology is about so much more than your Sun sign – and that the many different parts of your chart all work together to create the unique being that is you.

3

SEX AND YOUR
SUN SIGN

CANCER

(21 June–22 July)

Your polarity: Receptive
Your element: Water
Your modality: Cardinal
Your planetary ruler: The Moon
Your symbol: The Crab

WHAT CAN YOUR SUN SIGN TELL YOU ABOUT YOUR SEX LIFE?

Your Sun sign describes your basic identity and life's path – and, of course, sex plays into that! While we'd want to look at your entire birth chart, particularly your Venus and Mars signs, to get a more individualised idea of your sexual desires, your Sun sign gives us enough to start with.

So, how do we get from the Sun to between the sheets? First and most importantly, there's the sign's personality traits and how they might show up in your sex life. We know that Geminis are talkative, so it only follows that they'd be into dirty talk. We know that Leos love to be the centre of attention, so it makes complete sense that they'd have an exhibitionist streak.

Then there's each sign's body part. Um, what? Each sign is traditionally associated with one or more body parts, and paying special attention to this body part can be a big turn-on for that sign. For example, Taurus rules the throat and neck, so they might like being consensually choked (with a safe word at the ready, if needed) – or they might simply enjoy having their neck kissed and nibbled.

Finally, we're looking at compatibility. Each sign has other signs it's traditionally compatible with – and signs it's not so compatible with. Instead of ranking signs by compatibility, however, we're looking at each pairing's strengths and weaknesses – because sometimes opposites attract, after all!

YOUR SEXUAL PROFILE

As you're a water sign ruled by the Moon, sex is an emotional experience for you. Now, that doesn't mean that you need to be in a relationship to enjoy sex with someone, but for you sex is about more than just the body; it's a whole-self experience. Although you might have multiple sex partners, you take every relationship seriously – whether it's a fling, a friend with benefits, a polyamorous paramour or a monogamous relationship, you honour your connection with the other person. You love being emotionally and physically close with your partner, so you prefer positions that give you lots of skin-to-skin contact and you're always up for a cuddle.

Foreplay

You love touching and being touched, Cancer. Whether it's cuddling, a massage, soaping each other up in the shower or holding your date's hand as you walk down the street, physical contact is super important to you. So is eye contact, especially if it's combined with physical contact.

For you, foreplay is just as important as sex itself. You could make out with your partner for hours on end! You want to touch and be touched everywhere, but you particularly love having your nipples played with or playing with your partner's nipples (or both).

Your Turn-ons

Cancer is represented by the Crab, plus – as we already mentioned – you're a water sign, so you're predisposed to enjoy shower sex, bathtub sex, sex on the beach, sex in a swimming pool, sex under a waterfall … if there's water involved, you're wet in more ways than one (or hard – you get it). Cancer rules the chest, breasts and stomach, so, as mentioned previously, you likely enjoy nipple play of some kind – whether that's gentle sucking, biting or nipple clamps. You love having your chest, breasts or stomach stroked, and any sex position that combines cuddling with sex floats your boat – like spooning or karezza, the gentle slow-sex method. Or think of morning sex, where you begin by spooning each other, then your hands wander lower and, before you know it, you're kicking off your morning with an orgasm or three.

You're also into oral sex, both giving and receiving – including at the same time. The symbol for Cancer looks like a 69, after all. You might also have a foot fetish, or at least feel sexy in stockings or high heels – your mythology is based on a Greek story about a crab who bit Heracles's foot. Your sign is known for taking care of others, so you're giving just as much – if not more – pleasure than you receive. You're a romantic, that's true, but in a dirty-romance-novel-you-read-in-the-tub kind of way, not in a kiss-at-the-end-credits-of-a-Disney-movie kind of way. You wouldn't say no to some princess-themed roleplay, though ... you're creative and love a good story.

Your Turn-offs

You hate anything that's impersonal – you want to connect with your partner, even if it's a one-night stand. Your hook-up had better focus on making you feel good just as much as you focus on them; detachment or selfishness is a major turn-off for you. You're also not one for quickies; you'd rather wait until you can take your time with each other.

SEX POSITIONS

Based on the various traits of your sign (the symbol,
the element, the personality traits, the reputation …
you get the idea), we've found some sex positions
for you – if you haven't already discovered them on
your own, that is! If they sound fun, give 'em a try –
you might just feel a cosmic connection.

69

Your symbol looks like a 69 for a reason, Cancer –
plus, you love giving and receiving oral, so why
not combine the two?

Face-sitting

You love to take care of your partners, Cancer, and this position lets you do just that. Alternatively, if you're on top, you get off on knowing how much they want to go down on you – not to mention how amazing it feels.

Missionary

You'd rather connect with your partner than twist your body into all sorts of weird, uncomfortable shapes. Missionary is a classic sex position for a reason! Plus, the giver can easily add in some nipple play – your fave thing.

Spooning

Spooning combines your two favourite things –
cuddling and sex. Perfect for fingering, handjobs,
vaginal or anal sex (or just foreplay, if you prefer), this
position is easily adjustable to your needs.

Classic Oral

You're all about pleasure, Cancer, and whether you're going down on your partner or vice versa, this oral sex position is simple and effective.

Kneeling fingering

*This variation on spooning gives you plenty of
full-body contact while letting your (or your partner's)
hands do their thing.*

Shower Sex

You're a water sign, so get to the water – ASAP!

Seated

This sex position gives you and your partner plenty of skin-to-skin contact and it's perfect for nipple play.

MASTURBATION TIPS

You feel at home in the water, Cancer, so add some masturbation to your shower or soak in the tub. There are plenty of waterproof sex-toy options – these are your friends. BTW, even if you're just on your bed, use lube – lots of it. It'll make everything feel slicker.

SEX TOYS

Pick up a waterproof clitoral vibe, or a glass or silicone dildo to use in the shower. You love nipple play, so try some nipple clamps. BTW, many sex toys – whether it's a bullet vibe or a sex toy that simulates oral sex – can also be a lot of fun on your nipples.

WHERE TO HAVE SEX

Sex on the beach is a cliché, sure, but it's a hot one ... so head to a private area and bring a towel to keep the sand out. If that's too much work, your bathtub will do.

WHEN TO HAVE SEX

Make sure your schedule's free during Cancer Season, or when the Moon, Mars or Venus is in your sign – except for when Mars or Venus is retrograde, that is!

New Moons are great times to try new sex positions, while Full Moons are times to emotionally connect with your partner through your go-to positions, desires and kinks. If this isn't enough for you, look to your fellow water signs (Scorpio and Pisces) – when the Sun (or

Moon, Mars or Venus) is in their sign, you can shine, too.

BUT WHAT ABOUT THE REST OF MY CHART?

If you'd like even more sexual insight, look up the sex traits for your Moon, Rising, Mercury, Venus and Mars signs – particularly your Mars sign, which rules sex and libido. If you have a stellium (AKA three or more planets in the same sign, see page 25), look up those traits, too.

Remember, sex isn't just about you (unless it's masturbation, in which case, you're the star of the one-person show). If you have a regular sex partner, look up their Sun sign's traits, too.

Here's a quick run-through of each sign's sexual traits:

Aries: Passionate and direct, Aries love sex that's fast, intense and, most of all, fun.

Taurus: Slow and steady Taureans like to take their time for maximum pleasure.

Gemini: Witty and verbal, Gemini loves exploring fantasies and getting creative with their partner.

Cancer: Romantic Cancereans want to connect physically and emotionally with their partners.

Leo: Ruled by the Sun, Leos feel like the centre of the Universe – they love being the centre of attention, too, and have an exhibitionist side.

Virgo: Represented by 'the virgin', Virgos seem innocent at first, but they're incredibly sensual and have a secret kinky side.

Libra: Ruled by Venus, Librans are flirtatious and

romantic. They have a fine-tuned aesthetic sensibility, so their lingerie is on-point and their sex toys are as gorgeous as they are functional.

Scorpio: Intense, secretive Scorpios take sex seriously – they form a passionate connection with their partners and love exploring fantasies and power play.

Sagittarius: Adventurous Sagittarians will try anything once! They crave variety and get bored of the same-old, same-old.

Capricorn: Bossy Capricorn is all about structure and achieving their goals – think scheduled sex, efficient orgasms and mastering every sex position in the book.

Aquarius: Eccentric Aquarius loves exploring new kinks, sex positions and high-tech sex toys –

they're about five years ahead of the rest of the zodiac when it comes to the latest sex trends.

Pisces: Romantic Pisceans prioritise their emotional bond with their partners and love slow, sweet sex. But, as the last sign of the zodiac, they're also wise and non-judgmental – and excited to help their partners explore new kinks and sex positions.

4

ALL ABOUT
COMPATIBILITY

Chances are, you've looked up your and your crush's compatibility at least once – and may have been disappointed if some random online site didn't call you compatible. The truth is, compatibility is a lot more complicated than your Sun signs – if your Sun signs aren't compatible but your Moon, Venus and Mars signs are, you're probably a really strong couple with an incredible sex life. But even if your whole chart is incompatible, astrological tension doesn't necessarily mean you're doomed – just that you're different. And sometimes those differences can be super hot ... or at least make for mind-blowing hate-sex.

If you want a detailed look at your compatibility with your partner, you'll need a synastry reading, which is when a professional astrologer studies the details of both your birth charts and how they relate to each other. They're not just looking for the signs each of your planets are in, but the angles your charts make with each other, too.

By the way, ever heard of a little thing called free will? Although astrology might predict which areas of your relationship are particularly challenging, the choice to make up or break up comes down to you and your SO (though if you need something to blame it on, Mercury works just as well as the fact that they never wash the dishes).

Instead of ranking each couple from most compatible to most incompatible, the next pages outline the highs and lows of each potential pairing. Enjoy the good parts – and remember that you can work to find a compromise on your differences.

Cancer + Aries

You love taking care of your loved ones, Cancer, and as the baby of the zodiac, Aries loves to be taken care of. Aries thrives under Cancer's attention, but when things are bad, they're messy. Aries has a temper and a blunt nature that can sometimes accidentally (or not-so-accidentally) offend – while sensitive Cancer is easily hurt. And when Cancer is hurt, watch out for their crab claws!

Cancer + Taurus

Cancer and Taurus have a lot in common – they're homebodies who keep their loved ones close, and they pamper those they really care about. In a relationship, you'll spoil each other in the best way. But if you fight, watch out – Taurus is incredibly stubborn, while Cancer is moody, sensitive and will strike out with their crab claws if necessary.

Cancer + Gemini

Cancer loves to nurture their loved ones and, TBH, Gemini doesn't mind the attention. Both signs are creative in the bedroom, but Gemini is super social while Cancer tends to be withdrawn unless they're with someone they know well. Moody Gemini and sensitive Cancer are also likely to hurt each other's feelings, so they need to learn how to fight fair.

Cancer + Cancer

Two Cancers value the same thing in a relationship, have similar sex styles and just get each other. You're both homebodies who want to talk about your feelings in-between sex sessions. You're sweet and romantic with each other … until you're not. You're both moody and sensitive, so learn to talk out your issues instead of giving each other the cold shoulder.

Cancer + Leo

Cancer is ruled by the Moon and Leo by the Sun, so although you're very different, you're a natural pair. Cancer is introverted and loves to stay at home, while Leo is extroverted and loves to go out, but you're both creative, romantic and just a little bit (okay, a lot) dramatic. Cancer can feel neglected when Leo tends to their many fans, and Leo can get frustrated by Cancer's need for me time, but if you can learn to balance your needs, you can be a great pair.

Cancer + Virgo

You're both homebody signs and your place is probably both impeccably clean and beautifully decorated. Virgo is extremely logical, while Cancer leads with the heart, so you two can misunderstand each other and Virgo's perfectionism and criticism can hurt Cancer's feelings. But you both have a romantic streak, which can make up for a lot.

Cancer + Libra

You're both creative signs, and you value each other's sense of style and knowledge of the arts.

You could spend all day at the museum together ... and then follow it up with a hot evening in bed. However, air sign Libra can seem superficial and non-committal to emotional Cancer, while Libra can find the Crab too clingy. If you can respect each other's needs and boundaries, especially when you first start dating, you can make it work.

Cancer + Scorpio

As two water signs, you have a lot in common, and you have a similar approach to sex and relationships – when you fall, you fall hard, and you want a deep connection with your partner, whether it's a one-time fling or the love of your life. You understand each other well, but neither of you is at your best in a fight – Cancer is moody and sensitive, while Scorpio can put up walls and hold grudges like no other.

Cancer + Sagittarius

Cancer and Sagittarius are very different signs, but you can make up for what the other lacks. Adventurous Sagittarius can encourage Cancer to come out of their crab shell, while homey Cancer can provide a steadiness that Sagittarius didn't know they needed. That's the best-case scenario. In the worst-case scenario, Cancer finds Sagittarius a blunt, careless flake, and Sagittarius finds Cancer to be a clingy mess.

Cancer + Capricorn

As opposites on the zodiac wheel, you're a good match. You both value stability and you both take care of your loved ones. You could make a beautiful home and life together, with a great sex life to boot. However, practical Capricorn doesn't have much of a romantic side, which Cancer craves, and Cancer's moods can get on Capricorn's nerves – so you'll have to work hard to understand each other.

Cancer + Aquarius

You're both incredibly creative signs, though you express your creativity in different ways – Cancer might cook a delicious meal or decorate the bedroom in a way that deserves to be on the cover of an interior design magazine, while Aquarius will create an app that you never knew you needed or make a sex toy that'll blow Cancer's mind. However, Aquarius has a reputation for being a bit of a loner and the aloof Water-bearer could hurt romantic Cancer's feelings.

Cancer + Pisces

As two water signs, represented by the Crab and the Fish, you're a seemingly perfect pair – you're both romantic and creative, and you love love. However, you're both very emotional, which means that you might end up turning every little argument into a full-on nuclear war – so make sure you take some time to get in touch with reality before you confront each other.

ANOTHER WAY TO LOOK AT COMPATIBILITY

The stars tell you what you and your partner have in common, and where you're different – but attraction works in weird ways. Some people are attracted to those who share their exact same interests, style and goals, while others are drawn to those who are unlike themselves. So instead of asking what the stars say about you as a couple, ask yourself which zodiac sign sounds hottest to you. For example, if you're an Aries, you're astrologically compatible with Leos – but what if a life-of-the-party type sounds like the worst kind of match for you? Instead, ask yourself which zodiac archetype sounds most like your type – an emotional, dreamy Pisces? A logical, analytical Virgo? A fashionable, flirtatious Libra? Go back to page 27 and see which sign sounds like someone you'd want to date … or just fuck.

5

WHAT ASTROLOGY CAN (AND CAN'T) TELL YOU ABOUT YOUR SEX LIFE

Astrology is all about archetypes – traits and personality types that have been traditionally associated with each sign. When it comes to sex, astrology can tell us which signs you might vibe with, which parts of your body you love having touched and what sex styles and kinks you might be drawn to. Astrology can even predict the role romantic relationships will play in your life – if you'll date your way around the world or get married at a young age to the best friend you've known since you were five.

Astrology can make these guesses (and if you take your entire birth chart into account, those guesses become a lot more specific), but only you can decide if they're right. If you're an Aries but none of the Aries traits sound like you, you don't have to force yourself to fit them. You might personally relate more to another part of your birth chart, such as your Moon sign or Rising sign. Or you might defy categorisation entirely, because free will exists, after all.

Hopefully, this book has given you some sexy new ideas to try out, a new crush or two to consider and a sex toy suggestion that catches your eye. Try them all – but if you don't like them, that's totally okay. You'll have learned a little bit about yourself all the same.

6

THE ASTROSEX LIBRARY

If you'd like to learn more about astrology, here are some books, podcasts, apps, websites and Instagram accounts I recommend:

BOOKS

You Were Born for This by Chani Nicholas (Yellow Kite, 2020)

Astrology for Real Relationships by Jessica Lanyadoo (Crown Books, 2019)

Astrology for Happiness and Success by Mecca Woods (Adams Media, 2018)

The Astrology of Love & Sex by Annabel Gat (Chronicle Books, 2019)

Astro Poets: Your Guides to the Zodiac by Alex
   Dimitrov and Dorothea Lasky (Picador, 2019)
Astrology for Relationships by Jake Register
   (Rockridge Press, 2020)
Queer Cosmos by Colin Bedell (Cleis Press, 2020)

PODCASTS

Ghost of a Podcast
Stars Like Us: Astrology with Aliza Kelly

APPS

TimePassages
Sanctuary
The Pattern
Moon

WEBSITES

www.cafeastrology.com
www.astro.com
www.astro-seek.com
www.astrology.com
www.astro-charts.com

INSTAGRAM ACCOUNTS

@lisastardustastro
@queercosmos
@jakesastrology
@blackwomencry
@notallgeminis
@kayxstars
@lilithastrology
@solelunastro

GLOSSARY

Active: One of the two polarities (along with receptive) describing a sign's energy.

Ascendant: The zodiac sign that was on the horizon when you were born, representing the self you present to the world. Also called your Rising sign.

Aspect: The angle two planets or points make with each other in your birth chart, creating a certain type of energy.

Birth Chart: A snapshot of the cosmos at the exact moment you were born. Also called your natal chart.

Cardinal: One of the three modalities, describing signs that fall at the beginning of a season.

Conjunction: When two planets are very close together in the same sign.

Detriment: The sign in which a planet's influence is least powerful.

Domicile: The sign in which a planet feels most at home.

Element: One way to group the signs, describing whether they're associated with fire, earth, air or water.

Exaltation: The sign in which a planet feels particularly comfortable.

Essential Dignity: A way to describe how a planet 'feels' in a particular sign.

Fall: The sign in which a planet feels particularly uncomfortable.

Fixed: One of the three modalities, describing signs that fall in the middle of a season.

Generational Planets: The three outer planets – Uranus, Neptune and Pluto. They stay in a single sign for years, affecting entire generations.

Houses: The 12 sections of your birth chart, each describing a general area of life.

Mercury Retrograde: The much-hyped period of time when Mercury appears to move backwards in its orbit from our point of view on Earth, causing miscommunications, technological glitches and travel mishaps … and bringing our exes back.

Modality: One way to group the signs, describing where they fall in a season. The three modalities are cardinal, fixed and mutable.

Moon Sign: The sign the Moon was in when you were born, describing your emotions, needs and subconscious thoughts and desires.

Mutable: One of the three modalities, describing signs that fall at the end of a season.

Natal Chart: A snapshot of the cosmos at the exact moment you were born. Also called your birth chart.

Natal Chart Rectification: The process in which an astrologer works with you to determine the unknown parts of your birth chart.

Nodes of Destiny: Two mathematical points determined by the angles between the Sun, Moon and Earth when you were born. The North Node represents what we need to work on for spiritual growth, and the South Node represents the areas of life that come to us more easily.

Noon Chart: A birth chart calculated by using noon as the birth time, giving you an 'average' of where the planets and signs may have been. This is one way people who don't know their birth time can determine a birth chart.

Ophiuchus: A constellation in the sky that, no matter what the viral story of the day tells you, is not actually part of the zodiac.

Opposition: Planets that are 180 degrees apart, or six signs apart – they're opposite each other on the zodiac wheel. In an opposition, the two planets work against each other, as if they're playing tug-of-war.

Personal Planets: The Sun, Moon, Mercury, Venus and Mars. These planets change signs frequently (between every few days and every few months) and describe various aspects of your personality and day-to-day life.

Polarities: One way to describe signs' energies; there are two polarities, active and receptive.

Quincux: Two planets that are 150 degrees apart.

Receptive: One of the two polarities (along with active) describing a sign's energy.

Retrograde: When a planet appears to move backwards in its orbit from our point of view on Earth.

Ruler: A special relationship between a planet and a sign, or a sign and a house.

Rising Sign: The zodiac sign that was on the horizon when you were born, representing the self you present to the world. Also called your Ascendant.

Sextile: Planets that are 60 degrees apart, or two signs away from each other.

Square: Planets that are 90 degrees apart, or three signs away from each other.

Trine: Planets that are 120 degrees apart, or four signs away from each other.

Social Planets: Jupiter and Saturn. Falling between the personal planets and generational planets, these two planets change signs once every one to three years and represent bigger-picture themes than the personal planets.

Sun Sign: The sign the Sun was in when you were born, determining your identity and life purpose. Also called your 'star sign' your 'zodiac sign' or just your 'sign'.

Star Sign: Another term for 'Sun sign' describing which sign the Sun was in when you were born.

Stellium: When you have three or more planets in the same sign.

ABOUT THE AUTHOR

Erika W. Smith is a writer and editor based in Brooklyn, New York. She's written on astrology and sex for several publications, including *Refinery29* and *BUST* magazine, and is a Scorpio Sun, Sagittarius Moon, Virgo Rising.

You can follow her on Twitter and Instagram @erikawynn.